let's cook

indian

Shehzad Husain

p

Contents

Lamb Curry in a Thick Sauce

Originally a Kashmiri dish, this lamb stew is now made all over India and is popular wherever Indian food is eaten. Noted for its delicious tomato-flavoured sauce, it is ideal for a dinner party.

Serves 6

INGREDIENTS

1 kg/2 lb 4 oz lean lamb, with or without bone
7 tbsp yogurt
75 g/2³/4 oz/5 tbsp almonds
2 tsp garam masala
2 tsp fresh ginger root, finely chopped

2 tsp fresh garlic, crushed
1¹/2 tsp chilli powder
1¹/2 tsp salt
300 ml/¹/2 pint/1¹/4 cups oil
3 onions, finely chopped
4 green cardamoms

2 bay leaves
3 green chillies, chopped
2 tbsp lemon juice
400 g/14 oz can tomatoes
300 ml/¹/2 pint/1¹/4 cups water
fresh coriander (cilantro) leaves, chopped

1 Using a very sharp knife, cut the lamb into small, even-sized pieces.

2 In a large mixing bowl, combine the yogurt, almonds, garam masala, ginger, garlic, chilli powder and salt, stirring to mix well.

3 Heat the oil in a large saucepan and fry the onions with the cardamoms and the bay leaves until golden brown, stirring constantly.

4 Add the meat and the yogurt mixture to the pan and stir-fry for 3-5 minutes.

5 Add 2 green chillies, the lemon juice and the canned tomatoes to the mixture in the pan and stir-fry for a further 5 minutes.

6 Add the water to the pan, cover and leave to simmer over a low heat for 35-40 minutes.

7 Add the remaining green chilli and the coriander

(cilantro) leaves and stir until the sauce has thickened. (Remove the lid and turn the heat higher if the sauce is too watery.)

8 Transfer the curry to warm serving plates and serve hot.

Cauliflower with Meat

I love vegetables cooked with meat, especially cauliflower and spinach, which have a lovely flavour cooked this way. I use only a few spices but I like to add a baghaar *(seasoned oil dressing) at the end.*

Serves 4

INGREDIENTS

1 medium cauliflower
2 green chillies
300 ml/^{1}/2 pint/1^1/4 cups oil
2 onions, sliced
450 g/1 lb cubed lamb
1^1/2 tsp fresh ginger root, finely
  chopped

1^1/2 tsp fresh garlic, crushed
1 tsp chilli powder
1 tsp salt
fresh coriander (cilantro) leaves,
  chopped
850 ml/1^1/2 pints/3^3/4 cups water
1 tbsp lemon juice

BAGHAAR:
150 ml/^{1}/4 pint/^{2}/3 cup oil
4 dried red chillies
1 tsp mixed mustard and
  onion seeds

1 Using a sharp knife, cut the cauliflower into small florets. Chop the green chillies finely.

2 Heat the oil in a large saucepan. Add the onions and fry until golden brown.

3 Reduce the heat and add the meat, stirring.

4 Add the ginger, garlic, chilli powder and salt. Stir-fry for about 5 minutes, stirring to mix.

5 Add 1 green chilli and half of the coriander (cilantro) leaves.

6 Stir in the water and cook, covered, over a low heat for about 30 minutes.

7 Add the cauliflower and simmer for a further 15-20 minutes or until the water has evaporated completely. Stir-fry the mixture for another 5 minutes. Remove the pan from the heat and sprinkle the lemon juice sparingly.

8 To make the *baghaar*, heat the remaining oil in a separate small saucepan. Add the dried red chillies and the mixed mustard and onion seeds and fry until they turn a darker colour, stirring occasionally. Remove the pan from the heat and pour the mixture over the cooked cauliflower.

9 Garnish with the remaining green chilli and fresh coriander (cilantro) leaves. Serve immediately.

Meatballs in Sauce

*This is an old family recipe. The koftas (meatballs) are easy
to make and also freeze beautifully.*

Serves 4

INGREDIENTS

450 g/1 lb minced lamb
1 tsp fresh ginger root, crushed
1 tsp fresh garlic, crushed
1 tsp garam masala
1$^{1}/_{2}$ tsp poppy seeds
1 tsp salt
$^{1}/_{2}$ tsp chilli powder
1 medium onion, finely chopped
1 green chilli, finely chopped
fresh coriander (cilantro) leaves

1 tbsp gram flour
150 ml/$^{1}/_{4}$ pint/$^{2}/_{3}$ cup oil

SAUCE:
2 tbsp oil
3 medium onions, finely chopped
2 small cinnamon sticks
2 large black cardamoms
1 tsp fresh ginger root, finely
  chopped

1 tsp fresh garlic, crushed
1 tsp salt
75 ml/3 fl oz/4$^{1}/_{2}$ tbsp natural yogurt
150 ml/$^{1}/_{4}$ pint/$^{2}/_{3}$ cup water

TO GARNISH:
fresh coriander (cilantro) leaves,
  finely chopped
1 green chilli, finely chopped

1 Place the lamb in a large
mixing bowl.

2 Add the ginger, garlic, garam
masala, poppy seeds, salt,
chilli powder, onion, chilli,
coriander (cilantro) and gram
flour and mix well with a fork.

3 Make small meatballs out of
the mixture with your hands
and set aside.

4 To make the sauce, heat the
oil and fry the onions until
golden brown. Add the cinnamon
sticks and cardamoms to the pan,
lower the heat and stir-fry for a
further 5 minutes. Add the ginger,
garlic, salt and yogurt and stir
to mix well.

5 Transfer to a serving bowl
and garnish with chopped
coriander (cilantro) and chillies.

6 Heat the oil and fry
the meatballs, turning
occasionally, for 8-10 minutes or
until golden.

7 Transfer the meatballs to
warm serving plates. Serve
with the sauce and Chapatis.

Lamb Biryani

Cooked on festive occasions, especially for wedding, lamb biryani is amongst the most popular dishes in India. The meat can be cooked in advance and added to the rice on the day of the party.

Serves 4-6

INGREDIENTS

150 ml/¼ pint/⅔ cup milk
1 tsp saffron
5 tbsp ghee
3 medium onions, sliced
1 kg/2 lb 5 oz lean lamb, cubed
7 tbsp natural yogurt
1½ tsp fresh ginger root, finely chopped

1½ tsp fresh garlic, crushed
2 tsp garam masala
2 tsp salt
¼ tsp turmeric
600 ml/1 pint/2½ cups water
450 g/1 lb/2¼ cups basmati rice
2 tsp black cumin seeds
3 cardamoms

4 tbsp lemon juice
2 fresh green chillies
¼ bunch fresh coriander (cilantro) leaves

1 Boil the milk in a pan with the saffron and set aside. Heat the ghee in a pan and fry the onions until golden. Remove half of the onions and ghee from the pan and set aside in a bowl.

2 Combine the meat, yogurt, ginger, garlic, garam masala, 1 tsp salt and turmeric in a large bowl and mix well.

3 Return the pan with the ghee and onions to the heat, add the meat mixture, stir for about 3 minutes and add the water. Cook over a low heat for 45 minutes, stirring occasionally. Check to see whether the meat is tender: if not, add 150 ml/¼ pint/⅔ cup water and cook for 15 minutes. Once all the water has evaporated, stir-fry for about 2 minutes and set aside.

4 Meanwhile, place the rice in a pan. Add the cumin seeds, cardamoms, salt and enough water for cooking, and cook over a medium heat until the rice is half-cooked. Drain. Remove half of the rice and place in a bowl.

5 Spoon the meat mixture on top of the rice in the pan. Add half each of the saffron mixture, lemon juice, chillies and coriander (cilantro). Add the other half of the rice, saffron, lemon juice, chillies and coriander (cilantro). Cover and cook over a low heat for 15-20 minutes or until the rice is cooked. Stir well and serve hot.

Spicy Lamb Curry in Sauce

This curry is especially good served with plain boiled rice and Onion Dhaal.
Tamarind is traditionally used for this recipe but I like to use lemon juice.

Serves 4

INGREDIENTS

2 tsp ground cumin

2 tsp ground coriander

2 tsp desiccated (shredded) coconut

1 tsp mixed mustard and onion seeds

2 tsp sesame seeds

1 tsp fresh ginger root, finely chopped

1 tsp fresh garlic, crushed

1 tsp chilli powder

1 tsp salt

450 g/1 lb lean lamb

450 ml/16 fl oz/2 cups oil

3 medium onions, sliced

850 ml/1$\frac{1}{2}$ pints/3$\frac{3}{4}$ cups water

2 tbsp lemon juice

4 green chillies, split

1 Dry roast the ground cumin, ground coriander, desiccated (shredded) coconut, mixed mustard and onion seeds and the sesame seeds in a heavy frying pan (skillet), shaking the pan frequently to stop the spices from burning. Grind the roasted spices using a pestle and mortar.

2 In a large mixing bowl, blend together the roasted ground spices along with the ginger, garlic, chilli powder, salt and the cubed lamb and set aside.

3 In a separate pan, heat 300 ml/$\frac{1}{2}$ pint/1$\frac{1}{2}$ cups of the oil and fry the onions until golden brown.

4 Add the meat mixture to the onions and stir-fry for 5-7 minutes over a low heat. Add the water and simmer for 45 minutes, stirring occasionally. When the meat is cooked through, remove from the heat and sprinkle with the lemon juice.

5 In a separate saucepan, heat the remaining oil and add the

four split green chillies. Reduce the heat and cover with a lid. Remove the pan from the heat after about 30 seconds and set aside to cool.

6 Pour the chilli oil mixture over the meat curry and serve hot with Onion Dhaal and plain boiled rice.

Sliced Beef with Yogurt & Spices

There are many different ways of cooking this dish, but this is my particular favourite. However, for this recipe you need to roast the spices, as this helps give the dish a nice dark colour and a richer taste.

Serves 4

INGREDIENTS

450 g/1 lb lean beef slices, cut into
   2.5 cm/1-inch slices
5 tbsp yogurt
1 tsp fresh ginger root, finely
   chopped
1 tsp fresh garlic, crushed
1 tsp chilli powder
1 pinch turmeric

2 tsp garam masala
1 tsp salt
2 cardamoms
1 tsp black cumin seeds
50 g/1³/4 oz/¹/4 cup ground almonds
1 tbsp desiccated (shredded) coconut
1 tbsp poppy seeds
1 tbsp sesame seeds

300 ml/¹/2 pint/1¹/4 cups oil
2 medium onions, finely chopped
300 ml/¹/2 pint/1¹/4 cups water
2 green chillies
a few fresh coriander (cilantro)
   leaves, chopped

1 Place the beef in a large bowl, mix with the yogurt, ginger, garlic, chilli powder, turmeric, garam masala, salt, cardamoms and black cumin seeds and set aside until required.

2 Dry roast the ground almonds, desiccated (shredded) coconut, poppy seeds and sesame seeds in a heavy frying pan (skillet) until golden, shaking the pan to stop the spices from burning.

3 Work the spice mixture in a food processor until finely ground. (Add 1 tbsp of water to blend, if necessary.) Add the ground spice mixture to the meat mixture and combine.

4 Heat a little oil in a large saucepan and fry the onions until golden brown. Remove the onions from the pan. Stir-fry the meat in the remaining oil for about 5 minutes, then return the onions to the pan and stir-fry for a further 5-7 minutes. Add the water and leave to simmer over a low heat, covered, for 25-30 minutes, stirring occasionally. Add the green chillies and coriander (cilantro) leaves and serve hot.

VARIATION

Substitute lamb for the beef in this recipe, if you prefer.

Beef Khorma with Almonds

This khorma, *a traditional northern Indian recipe,*
has a thick sauce and is quite simple to cook.

Serves 6

INGREDIENTS

300 ml/^{1}/$_2$ pint/1^1/$_4$ cups oil
3 medium onions, finely chopped
1 kg/2 lb 4 oz lean beef, cubed
1^1/$_2$ tsp garam masala
1^1/$_2$ tsp ground coriander
1^1/$_2$ tsp fresh ginger root, finely
  chopped

1^1/$_2$ tsp fresh garlic, crushed
1 tsp salt
150 ml/5 fl oz/^{2}/$_3$ cup natural yogurt
2 cloves
3 green cardamoms
4 black peppercorns
600 ml/1 pint/2^1/$_2$ cups water

TO GARNISH:
6 almonds, soaked, peeled and
  chopped
2 green chillies, chopped
a few fresh coriander (cilantro) leaves

1 Heat the oil in a saucepan.
Add the onions and stir-fry
until golden brown. Remove half
of the onions from the pan, set
aside and reserve.

2 Add the meat to the
remaining onions in the pan
and stir-fry for about 5 minutes.
Remove the pan from the heat.

3 Mix the garam masala,
ground coriander, ginger,
garlic, salt and yogurt in a bowl.

Gradually add the meat to the
yogurt and spice mixture and mix
to coat the meat on all sides. Place
in the saucepan, return to the
heat, and stir for 5-7 minutes,
or until the mixture is nearly
brown in colour.

4 Add the cloves, green
cardamoms and black
peppercorns. Add the water, lower
the heat, cover and leave to
simmer for about 45-60 minutes.
If the water has completely

evaporated but the meat is still
not tender enough, add another
300 ml/^{1}/$_2$ pint/1^1/$_2$ cups water and
cook for a further 10-15 minutes,
stirring occasionally.

5 Just before serving, garnish
with the reserved onions,
chopped almonds, green chillies
and the fresh coriander (cilantro)
leaves.Serve with Chapatis.

Chicken Tikka

*For this very popular dish, small pieces of chicken are marinated
for a minimum of 3 hours in yogurt and spices.*

Serves 6

INGREDIENTS

1 tsp fresh ginger root, finely
 chopped
1 tsp fresh garlic, crushed
$^1/_2$ tsp ground coriander
$^1/_2$ tsp ground cumin
1 tsp chilli powder
3 tbsp yogurt

1 tsp salt
2 tbsp lemon juice
a few drops of red food colouring
 (optional)
1 tbsp tomato purée (paste)
1.5 kg/3 lb 5 oz chicken breast
1 onion, sliced

3 tbsp oil

TO GARNISH:
6 lettuce leaves
1 lemon, cut into wedges

1 Blend together the ginger, garlic, ground coriander, ground cumin and chilli powder in a large mixing bowl.

2 Add the yogurt, salt, lemon juice, red food colouring (if using) and the tomato purée (paste) to the spice mixture.

3 Using a sharp knife, cut the chicken into pieces. Add the chicken to the spice mixture and toss to coat well. Leave to

marinate for at least 3 hours, preferably overnight.

4 Arrange the onion in the bottom of a heatproof dish. Carefully drizzle half of the oil over the onions.

5 Arrange the marinated chicken pieces on top of the onions and cook under a pre-heated grill (broiler), turning once and basting with the remaining oil, for 25-30 minutes.

6 Serve the chicken tikka on a bed of lettuce and garnish with the lemon wedges.

COOK'S TIP

*Chicken Tikka can be served with
Naan Breads, Raita and Mango
Chutney or as a starter.*

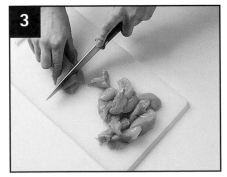

Chicken Khorma

Chicken khorma *is one of the most popular curries,*
and this one is perfect for a dinner party.

Serves 4-6

INGREDIENTS

1¹/₂ tsp fresh ginger root, finely
   chopped
1¹/₂ tsp fresh garlic, crushed
2 tsp garam masala
1 tsp chilli powder
1 tsp salt
1 tsp black cumin seeds

3 green cardamoms, with husks
   removed and seeds crushed
1 tsp ground coriander
1 tsp ground almonds
150 ml/5 fl oz/²/₃ cup natural yogurt
8 whole chicken breasts, skinned
300 ml/¹/₂ pint/1¹/₄ cups oil

2 medium onions, sliced
150 ml/¹/₄ pint/²/₃ cup water
fresh coriander (cilantro) leaves
green chillies, chopped
boiled rice, to serve

1 Mix the ginger, garlic, garam
masala, chilli powder, salt,
black cumin seeds, green
cardamoms, ground coriander and
almonds with the yogurt.

2 Spoon the yogurt and spice
mixture over the chicken
breasts and set aside to marinate.

3 Heat the oil in a large frying
pan (skillet). Add the onions
to the pan and fry until a golden
brown colour.

4 Add the chicken breasts to
the pan, stir-frying for
5-7 minutes.

5 Add the water, cover and leave
to simmer for 20-25 minutes.

6 Add the coriander (cilantro)
and green chillies and cook
for a further 10 minutes, stirring
gently from time to time.

7 Transfer to a serving plate and
serve with boiled rice.

VARIATION

Chicken portions may be used
instead of breasts, if preferred, and
should be cooked for 10 minutes
longer in step 5.

Tandoori-Style Chicken

In India, tandoori chicken is traditionally cooked in a tandoor (clay) oven. Alternatively, I pre-heat the grill (broiler) to a very high temperature then lower it to medium to cook this dish.

Serves 4

INGREDIENTS

8 chicken drumsticks, skinned
150 ml/5 fl oz/^{2}/$_3$ cup natural yogurt
1^1/$_2$ tsp fresh ginger root, finely chopped
1^1/$_2$ tsp fresh garlic, crushed
1 tsp chilli powder
2 tsp ground cumin

2 tsp ground coriander
1 tsp salt
^{1}/$_2$ tsp red food colouring
1 tbsp tamarind paste
150 ml/^{1}/$_4$ pint/^{2}/$_3$ cup water
150 ml/^{1}/$_4$ pint/^{2}/$_3$ cup oil
lettuce leaves, to serve

TO GARNISH:
onion rings
sliced tomatoes
lemon wedges

1 Make 2-3 slashes in each piece of chicken.

2 Place the yogurt in a bowl. Add the ginger, garlic, chilli powder, ground cumin, ground coriander, salt and red food colouring and blend together until well combined.

3 Add the chicken to the yogurt and spice mixture and mix to coat well. Leave the chicken to marinate in the refrigerator for a minimum of 3 hours.

4 In a separate bowl, mix the tamarind paste with the water and fold into the yogurt and spice mixture. Toss the chicken pieces in this mixture and set aside to marinate for a further 3 hours.

5 Transfer the chicken pieces to a heatproof dish and brush the chicken with oil. Cook the chicken under a pre-heated medium-hot grill (broiler) for 30-35 minutes, turning the chicken pieces occasionally and basting with the remaining oil.

6 Arrange the chicken on a bed of lettuce and garnish with onion rings, sliced tomatoes and lemon wedges.

COOK'S TIP

Serve the succulent chicken pieces on a bed of lettuce, and garnished with a few onion rings, sliced tomatoes and lemon wedges. Naan Bread and Mint Raita complement the dish perfectly.

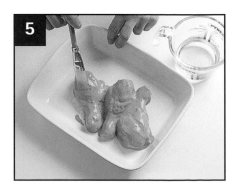

Chicken Jalfrezi

This is a quick and tasty way to use leftover roast chicken. The sauce can also be used for any cooked poultry, lamb or beef.

Serves 4

INGREDIENTS

1 tsp mustard oil
3 tbsp vegetable oil
1 large onion, chopped finely
3 garlic cloves, crushed
1 tbsp tomato purée (paste)
2 tomatoes, peeled and chopped
1 tsp ground turmeric

$^1/_2$ tsp cumin seeds, ground
$^1/_2$ tsp coriander seeds, ground
$^1/_2$ tsp chilli powder
$^1/_2$ tsp garam masala
1 tsp red wine vinegar
1 small red (bell) pepper, chopped

125 g/4 oz/1 cup frozen broad (fava) beans
500 g/1 lb cooked chicken breasts, cut into bite-sized pieces
salt
fresh coriander (cilantro) sprigs, to garnish

1 Heat the mustard oil in a large, frying pan (skillet) set over a high heat for about 1 minute until it begins to smoke. Add the vegetable oil, reduce the heat and then add the onion and the garlic. Fry the garlic and onion until they are golden.

2 Add the tomato purée (paste), chopped tomatoes, ground turmeric, cumin and coriander seeds, chilli powder, garam masala and red wine vinegar to the frying pan (skillet). Stir the mixture until fragrant.

3 Add the red (bell) pepper and broad (fava) beans and stir for 2 minutes until the (bell) pepper is softened. Stir in the chicken, and salt to taste. Leave to simmer gently for 6-8 minutes until the chicken is heated through and the beans are tender.

4 Serve garnished with coriander (cilantro) leaves.

COOK'S TIP

This dish is an ideal way of making use of leftover poultry – turkey, duck or quail. Any variety of beans works well, but vegetables are just as useful, especially root vegetables, courgettes (zucchini), potatoes or broccoli. Leafy vegetables will not be so successful.

Bengali-Style Fish

Fresh fish is eaten a great deal in Bengal (Bangladesh), and this dish is made with mustard oil which gives the fish a good flavour.

Serves 4–6

INGREDIENTS

1 tsp turmeric
1 tsp salt
1 kg/2 lb 4 oz cod fillet, skinned and
   cut into pieces
6 tbsp corn oil

4 green chillies
1 tsp fresh ginger root, finely
   chopped
1 tsp fresh garlic, crushed
2 medium onions, finely chopped

2 tomatoes, finely chopped
6 tbsp mustard oil
450 ml/³/₄ pint/2 cups water
fresh coriander (cilantro) leaves,
   chopped, to garnish

1 Mix together the turmeric and salt in a small bowl.

2 Spoon the turmeric and salt mixture over the fish pieces.

3 Heat the oil in a frying-pan (skillet). Add the fish to the pan and fry until pale yellow. Remove the fish with a perforated spoon and set aside.

4 Place the green chillies, ginger, garlic, onions and tomatoes in a pestle and mortar and grind to form a paste.

Alternatively, work the ingredients in a food processor.

5 Transfer the spice paste to a saucepan and dry-fry until golden brown.

6 Remove the pan from the heat and gently place the fish pieces into the paste without breaking the fish up.

7 Return the pan to the heat, add the water and cook the fish, uncovered, over a medium heat for 15-20 minutes.

8 Serve garnished with chopped coriander (cilantro).

COOK'S TIP

In the hot and humid eastern plains that surround Bengal, the mustard plant flourishes, providing oil for cooking and spicy seeds for flavouring. Fish and seafood appear in many meals, often flavoured with mustard oil.

Vegetable Kebabs (Kabobs)

If you invite several people to dinner or to a buffet meal nowadays there is a strong chance that one of them may be a vegetarian. These kebabs (kabobs) are easy to make and taste delicious.

Makes 10–12

INGREDIENTS

2 large potatoes, sliced
1 medium onion, sliced
$1/2$ medium cauliflower, cut into
   small florets
50 g/$1^3/4$ oz peas
1 tbsp spinach purée (paste)

2-3 green chillies
fresh coriander (cilantro) leaves
1 tsp fresh ginger root, finely
   chopped
1 tsp fresh garlic, crushed
1 tsp ground coriander

1 pinch turmeric
1 tsp salt
50 g/$1^3/4$ oz/1 cup breadcrumbs
300 ml/$1/2$ pint/$1^1/4$ cups oil
fresh chilli strips, to garnish

1 Place the potatoes, onion and cauliflower florets in a pan of water and bring to the boil. Reduce the heat and leave to simmer until the potatoes are cooked through. Remove the vegetables from the pan with a perforated spoon and drain thoroughly.

2 Add the peas and spinach to the vegetables and mix, mashing down with a fork.

3 Using a sharp knife, finely chop the green chillies and fresh coriander (cilantro) leaves.

4 Mix the chillies and coriander (cilantro) with the ginger, garlic, ground coriander, turmeric and salt.

5 Blend the spice mixture into the vegetables, mixing with a fork to make a paste.

6 Scatter the breadcrumbs on to a large plate.

7 Break off 10-12 small balls from the spice paste. Flatten them with the palm of your hand to make flat, round shapes.

8 Dip each kebab (kabob) in the breadcrumbs, coating well.

9 Heat the oil in a heavy frying-pan (skillet) and shallow-fry the kabobs (kabobs), in batches, until golden brown, turning occasionally. Transfer to serving plates and garnish with fresh chilli strips. Serve hot.

Vegetable Curry

This colourful and interesting mixture of vegetables, cooked in a spicy sauce, is excellent served with Pulao Rice and Naan Bread.

Serves

INGREDIENTS

250 g/8 oz turnips or swede, peeled
1 aubergine (eggplant), leaf end
 trimmed
350 g/12 oz new potatoes, scrubbed
250 g/8 oz cauliflower
250 g/8 oz button mushrooms
1 large onion
250 g/8 oz carrots, peeled
6 tbsp vegetable ghee or oil
2 garlic cloves, crushed

5 cm/2 inch ginger root, chopped
 finely
1-2 fresh green chillies, seeded and
 chopped
1 tbsp paprika
2 tsp ground coriander
1 tbsp mild or medium curry powder
 or paste
450 ml/³/4 pint/1³/4 cups vegetable
 stock

425 g/14 oz can chopped tomatoes
1 green (bell) pepper, seeded and
 sliced
1 tbsp cornflour (cornstarch)
150 ml/¹/4 pint/²/3 cup coconut milk
2-3 tbsp ground almonds
salt
fresh coriander (cilantro) sprigs, to
 garnish

1 Cut the turnips or swede, aubergine (eggplant) and potatoes into 1 cm/¹/2 inch cubes. Divide the cauliflower into small florets. Leave the mushrooms whole, or slice thickly if preferred. Slice the onion and carrots.

2 Heat the ghee or oil in a large saucepan, add the onion, turnip, potato and cauliflower and cook gently for 3 minutes, stirring frequently. Add the garlic, ginger, chillies, paprika, ground coriander and curry powder or paste and cook for 1 minute, stirring.

3 Add the stock, tomatoes, aubergine (eggplant) and mushrooms and season with salt. Cover and leave to simmer gently for about 30 minutes or until tender, stirring occasionally. Add the green (bell) pepper, cover and continue cooking for a further 5 minutes.

4 Smoothly blend the cornflour (cornstarch) with the coconut milk and stir into the mixture. Add the ground almonds and leave to simmer for 2 minutes, stirring all the time. Season if necessary. Transfer to serving plates and serve hot, garnished with sprigs of fresh coriander (cilantro).

Chick-pea (Garbanzo Bean) Curry

This curry is very popular amongst the many vegetarian people in India. There are many different ways of cooking chick-peas (garbanzo beans), but this version is probably one of the most delicious.

Serves 4

INGREDIENTS

6 tbsp oil
2 medium onions, sliced
1 tsp fresh ginger root, finely chopped
1 tsp ground cumin

1 tsp ground coriander
1 tsp fresh garlic, crushed
1 tsp chilli powder
2 fresh green chillies
fresh coriander (cilantro) leaves

150 ml/$\frac{1}{4}$ pint/$\frac{2}{3}$ cup water
1 large potato
400 g/14 oz can chick-peas (garbanzo beans), drained
1 tbsp lemon juice

1 Heat the oil in a large saucepan.

2 Add the onions to the pan and fry, stirring occasionally, until golden brown.

3 Reduce the heat, add the ginger, ground cumin, ground coriander, garlic, chilli powder, fresh green chillies and fresh coriander (cilantro) leaves to the pan and stir-fry for 2 minutes.

4 Add the water to the mixture in the pan and stir to mix.

5 Using a sharp knife, cut the potato into small dice.

6 Add the potatoes and the drained chick peas to the mixture in the pan, cover and leave to simmer, stirring occasionally, for 5-7 minutes.

7 Sprinkle the lemon juice over the curry.

8 Transfer the chick pea curry to serving dishes. Serve the curry hot with chapati, if you wish.

COOK'S TIP

Using canned chick-peas (garbanzo beans) saves time, but you can use dried chick-peas (garbanzo beans) if you prefer. Soak them overnight, then boil them for 15-20 minutes or until soft.

Onion Dhaal

This dhaal *is semi-dry when cooked so it is best to serve it with a curry which has a sauce. Ordinary onions can be used as a substitute if spring onions (scallions) are not available.*

Serves 4

INGREDIENTS

100 g/3$^{1}/_{2}$ oz/$^{1}/_{2}$ cup *masoor dhaal*
6 tbsp oil
1 small bunch spring onions (scallions), trimmed and chopped,, including the green part

1 tsp fresh ginger root, finely chopped
1 tsp fresh garlic, crushed
$^{1}/_{2}$ tsp chilli powder
$^{1}/_{2}$ tsp turmeric

300 ml/$^{1}/_{2}$ pint/1$^{1}/_{4}$ cups water
1 tsp salt
1 fresh green chilli, finely chopped
fresh coriander (cilantro) leaves

1 Rinse the lentils and set aside until required.

2 Heat the oil in a saucepan. Add the spring onions (scallions) to the pan and fry until lightly browned.

3 Reduce the heat and add the ginger, garlic, chilli powder and turmeric to the pan. Stir-fry the spring onions (scallions) with the spices.

4 Add the lentils and mix to blend together.

5 Add the water to the lentil mixture in the pan, reduce the heat further and cook for 20-25 minutes.

6 When the lentils are cooked thoroughly, add the salt and stir with a wooden spoon to gently combine.

7 Garnish the onion lentils with the chopped green chillies and fresh coriander (cilantro) leaves. Transfer the onion lentils to a serving dish and serve immediately.

COOK'S TIP

Masoor dhaal *are small, round, pale orange split lentils. They turn a pale yellow colour when cooked.*

Pulao Rice

Plain boiled rice is eaten by most people in India every day, but for entertaining we tend to choose a more interesting rice dish, such as this one which has different-coloured grains and spices in it.

Serves 2-4

INGREDIENTS

200 g/7 oz/1 cup basmati rice
2 tbsp ghee
3 green cardamoms
2 cloves

3 peppercorns
1/2 tsp salt
1/2 tsp saffron

400 ml/3/4 pint/2 cups water

1 Rinse the rice twice and set aside until required.

2 Heat the ghee in a saucepan. Add the cardamoms, cloves and peppercorns to the pan and fry, stirring, for about 1 minute.

3 Add the rice and stir-fry for a further 2 minutes.

4 Add the salt, saffron and water to the rice mixture and reduce the heat. Cover the pan and leave to simmer over a low heat until the water has evaporated.

5 Transfer to a serving dish and serve hot.

COOK'S TIP

The most expensive of all spices, saffron strands are the stamens of a type of crocus. They give dishes a rich, golden colour, as well as adding a distinctive, slightly bitter taste. Saffron is sold as a powder or in strands. Saffron strands are more expensive, but do have a superior flavour. Some books recommend substituting turmeric – although the colours are similar, the tastes are not.

COOK'S TIP

Cloves should be used with caution because the flavour can be overwhelming if too many are used.

Naan Bread

There are many ways of making naan bread, but this particular recipe is very easy to follow.
Naan bread should be served warm, preferably immediately after cooking.

Makes 6-8

INGREDIENTS

1 tsp sugar
1 tsp fresh yeast
150 ml/^{1}/$_4$ pint/^{2}/$_3$ cup warm water

200 g/7 oz/1^1/$_2$ cups plain (all-purpose) flour
1 tbsp ghee

1 tsp salt
50 g/1^3/$_4$ oz/6 tbsp unsalted butter
1 tsp poppy seeds

1 Put the sugar and yeast in a small bowl or jug with the warm water and mix well until the yeast has dissolved. Set aside for about 10 minutes or until the mixture is frothy.

2 Place the flour in a large mixing bowl. Make a well in the middle of the flour, add the ghee and salt and pour in the yeast mixture. Mix well to form a dough, using your hands and adding more water if required.

3 Turn the dough out on to a floured surface and knead for about 5 minutes or until smooth.

4 Return the dough to the bowl, cover and leave to rise in a warm place for 1½ hours or until doubled in size.

5 Turn the dough out on to a floured surface and knead for a further 2 minutes. Break off small balls with your hand and pat them into rounds about 12 cm/ 5 inches in diameter and 1 cm/ ½ inch thick.

6 Place the dough rounds on to a greased sheet of foil and grill (broil) under a very hot pre-heated grill (broiler) for 7-10 minutes, turning twice and brushing with the butter and sprinkling with the poppy seeds.

7 Serve warm immediately, or keep wrapped in foil until required.

COOK'S TIP

A tandoor oven throws out a ferocious heat; this bread is traditionally cooked on the side wall of the oven where the heat is only slightly less than in the centre. For an authentic effect, leave your grill (broiler) on for a long time to heat up before the first dough goes under.

Chapati

This is one of the less fattening Indian breads because it contains no fat, but some people like to brush them with a little melted butter before serving.

Makes 10-12

INGREDIENTS

225 g/8 oz/1 1/2 cups wholemeal flour (*ata* or *chapati* flour)

1/2 tsp salt

200 ml/1/3 pint/3/4 cup water

1 Place the flour in a large mixing bowl. Add the salt and mix to combine.

2 Make a well in the middle of the flour and gradually pour in the water, mixing well with your fingers to form a supple dough.

3 Knead the dough for about 7-10 minutes. Ideally, set the dough aside and leave to rise for about 15-20 minutes, but if time is short roll out the dough straightaway. Divide the dough into 10-12 equal portions. Roll out each piece of dough on a well-floured surface.

4 Place a heavy-based frying-pan (skillet) on a high heat. When steam starts to rise from the frying pan (skillet), lower the heat to medium.

5 Place a chapati in the frying pan (skillet) and when the chapati starts to bubble turn it over. Carefully press down on the chapati with a clean tea towel (dishcloth) or a flat spoon and turn the chapati over once again. Remove the chapati from the pan, set aside and keep warm while you make the others.

6 Repeat the process until all of the chapatis are cooked.

COOK'S TIP

Ideally, chapatis should be eaten as they come out of the frying pan (skillet), but if that is not practical keep them warm after cooking by wrapping them up in foil. In India, chapatis are sometimes cooked on a naked flame, which makes them puff up. Allow about 2 per person.

Pakoras

Pakoras are eaten all over India. They are made in many different ways and with a variety of fillings. Sometimes they are served in yogurt.

Serves 4

INGREDIENTS

6 tbsp gram flour
$^1/_2$ tsp salt
1 tsp chilli powder
1 tsp baking powder
$1^1/_2$ tsp white cumin seeds

1 tsp pomegranate seeds
300 ml/$^1/_2$ pint/$1^1/_4$ cups water
fresh coriander (cilantro) leaves,
   finely chopped

vegetables of your choice:
   cauliflower, cut into small florets,
   onions, cut into rings, potatoes,
   sliced, aubergines (eggplants),
   sliced, or fresh spinach leaves)
oil, for deep-frying

1 Sift the gram flour into a large mixing bowl.

2 Add the salt, chilli powder, baking powder, cumin and pomegranate seeds and blend together well.

3 Pour in the water and beat well to form a smooth batter.

4 Add the coriander (cilantro) and mix. Set the batter aside.

5 Dip the prepared vegetables of your choice into the batter, carefully shaking off any of the excess batter.

6 Heat the oil in a large heavy-based pan. Place the battered vegetables of your choice in the oil and deep-fry, in batches, turning once.

7 Repeat this process until all of the batter has been used up.

8 Transfer the battered vegetables to kitchen paper and drain thoroughly. Serve immediately.

COOK'S TIP

When deep-frying, it is important to use oil at the correct temperature. If the oil is too hot, the outside of the food will burn as will the spices, before the inside is cooked. If the oil is too cool, the food will be sodden with oil before a crisp batter forms. Draining on kitchen paper is essential as it absorbs excess oil and moisture.

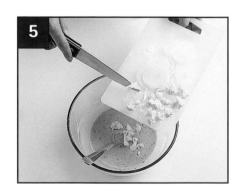

Samosas

Samosas, which are a sort of Indian Cornish pasty, make excellent snacks. In India you can buy them along the roadside, and they are very popular. They are may be frozen and re-heated.

Makes 10–12

INGREDIENTS

PASTRY:
100 g/3^1/2 oz/^{3}/4 cup self-raising flour
^{1}/2 tsp salt
40 g/1^1/2 oz/3 tbsp butter, cut into small pieces
4 tbsp water

FILLING:
3 medium potatoes, boiled
1 tsp fresh ginger root, finely chopped
1 tsp fresh garlic, crushed
^{1}/2 tsp white cumin seeds
^{1}/2 tsp mixed onion and mustard seeds

1 tsp salt
^{1}/2 tsp crushed red chillies
2 tbsp lemon juice
2 small green chillies, finely chopped
ghee or oil, for deep-frying

1 Sift the flour and salt into a large mixing bowl. Add the butter and rub into the flour until the mixture resembles fine breadcrumbs.

2 Pour in the water and mix with a fork to form a dough. Pat the dough into a ball and knead for 5 minutes or until the dough is smooth. Add a little flour if the dough is sticky. Cover and leave to rise.

3 To make the filling, mash the boiled potatoes gently and mix with the ginger, garlic, white cumin seeds, onion and mustard seeds, salt, crushed red chillies, lemon juice and green chilli.

4 Break small balls off the dough and roll each out very thinly to form a round. Cut in half, dampen the edges and shape into cones. Fill the cones with a little of the filling, dampen the top and bottom edges of the cones and pinch together to seal Set aside.

5 Fill a deep pan one-third full with oil and heat to 180°-190°C/350°-375°F or until a small cube of bread browns in 30 seconds. Carefully lower the samosas into the oil, a few at a time, and fry for 2-3 minutes or until golden brown. Remove from the oil and drain thoroughly on kitchen towels. Serve hot or cold.

Raitas

Raitas are very easy to prepare, very versatile and have a cooling effect which will be appreciated if you are serving hot, spicy dishes.

Serves 4

INGREDIENTS

MINT RAITA:

200 ml/7 fl oz/³/₄ cup natural yogurt
50 ml/2 fl oz/4 tbsp water
1 small onion, finely chopped
¹/₂ tsp mint sauce
¹/₂ tsp salt
3 fresh mint leaves, to garnish

CUCUMBER RAITA:

225 g/8 oz cucumber
1 medium onion
¹/₂ tsp salt
¹/₂ tsp mint sauce
300 ml/10 fl oz/1¹/₄ cups yogurt
150 ml/¹/₄ pint/²/₃ cup water
fresh mint leaves, to garnish

AUBERGINE (EGGPLANT) RAITA:

1 medium aubergine (eggplant)
1 tsp salt
1 small onion, finely chopped
2 green chillies, finely chopped
200 ml/7 fl oz/³/₄ cup natural yogurt
3 tbsp water

1 To make the mint raita, place the yogurt in a bowl and whisk with a fork. Gradually add the water, whisking well. Add the onion, mint sauce and salt and blend together. Garnish with the fresh mint leaves.

2 To make the cucumber raita, peel and slice the cucumber. Using a sharp knife, chop the onion finely. Place the cucumber and onion in a large bowl, then add the salt and the mint sauce. Add the yogurt and the water and place the mixture in a liquidizer and blend well. Transfer to a serving bowl and serve garnished with a few fresh mint leaves.

3 To make the aubergine (eggplant) raita, rinse the aubergine (eggplant) and remove the top end. Discard the top and chop the rest into small pieces. Boil the aubergine (eggplant) in a pan of water until soft and mushy. Drain the aubergine (eggplant) and mash. Transfer to a serving bowl and add the salt, the onion and green chillies, mixing well. Whip the yogurt with the water in a separate bowl and pour over the aubergine (eggplant) mixture. Mix well and serve.

This is a Parragon Book
First published in 2003

Parragon
Queen Street House
4 Queen Street, Bath, BA1 1HE, UK

ISBN: 1-40540-824-3

Printed in China

NOTE

This book uses imperial and metric measurements. Follow the same units
of measurement throughout; do not mix imperial and metric. All spoon
measurements are level; teaspoons are assumed to be 5 ml and
tablespoons are assumed to be 15 ml. Unless otherwise stated, milk is
assumed to be whole milk, eggs and individual vegetables such as
potatoes are medium, and pepper is freshly ground black pepper.

The times given for each recipe are an approximate guide only because
the preparation times may differ according to the techniques used by
different people and the cooking times may vary as a result of the type of
oven used.

Recipes using raw or very lightly cooked eggs should be avoided by
infants, the elderly, pregnant women, convalescents and anyone suffering
from an illness.